THE HANDS OF TIME

The Hands of Time

Darrell F. Litsinger

Copyright © 2010 by Darrell F. Litsinger.

ISBN: Hardcover   978-1-4500-3765-5
       Softcover   978-1-4500-3764-8

All rights reserved. No part of this book may be reproduced or transmitted in any form or by any means, electronic or mechanical, including photocopying, recording, or by any information storage and retrieval system, without permission in writing from the copyright owner.

This book was printed in the United States of America.

To order additional copies of this book, contact:
Xlibris Corporation
1-888-795-4274
www.Xlibris.com
Orders@Xlibris.com
58597

Contents

Prologue 9
Center Stage 11
The Great Depression 14
Uncle Sam Sends Greetings 22
Camp Cooke 24
Hawaii Bound 26
We Sail Into . . . . ? 30
Destination . . . . Okinawa 33
We Land On Purple Beach 35
Day Two 37
The Rainy Season 40
The End Is Near 45
The War's End 46
Naha Airfield 47
Korea Bound 51
The Last Big Sweat . . . . And Out! 54
Home At Last 60
Our Marriage 62
Epilogue 67

DEDICATION

To my parents, Joseph E. and Clara E. for all their sacrifices through the years while providing for me and teaching me the good things of life.

Prologue

This has been an interesting experience, writing about myself and my goings and comings. I trust that the reader will enjoy it and experience the activities of my lifestyle. It has always been my desire to write and in doing so, I have experienced the satisfaction of this purpose. This involves the "Greatest Generation", my membership in it and our activities during these years. It was, to say the least, a time of trials and many problems. May the reader enjoy these words and hope and pray that they do not ever need to experience many of these activities as I did.

Center Stage

Sometime during the month of April 1922, Clara Litsinger approached Joe, her husband, with this rather alarming news:

"Joe, guess what, I'm pregnant".

Joe, although preoccupied with his accounts for the next days run, listened, but not the way he should have.

Clara reviewed her thoughts and again said, "Joe, listen to me, I'm pregnant".

Joe Litsinger took a step backward, sat down in a chair nearby, looked surprised and exclaimed, "How could that happen"?

Clara, with some haste told him very firmly, "You must surely know 'how it happened'. Remember the night that we had guests at the house and I could not get to the bathroom for you know what. We cannot backtrack now, its time for serious thinking. In addition, I gave away all of my baby blankets and other things. Oh Joe, what will women say, no one that I know, my age, are having babies".

Joe tried to collect his thoughts, but the thoughts he had were something akin to paying bills, getting up all hours of the night, washing diapers, getting the back bedroom ready for a new occupant and above all, telling their son Homer, that he was going to have a new sister or brother.

Needless to say, the months rolled by and I arrived on schedule, somewhere around midnight on the 3rd day of January 1923. My father, stood at the foot of the bed, while not helping with LaMaize, as they do today, but at least praying and giving Clara and me all the attention he could muster. Ole Doc Kessler did the necessary things to help things along and Clara, indeed, did more than her share. I came out bawling my head off, a big 8-pound, blue eyed, hunk of baby flesh, ready to take on the world. This was it man. "I'm here, everybody take notice, this is ME".

Well, I must tell you this. My mother, Clara, was prepared for a girl and had already selected a girls name . . . I was supposed to be named "Louise". However, her plans were changed in a matter of several minutes . . . . I was named "Darrell". Someone had mentioned that name to her and that was it.

Very soon after, I was introduced to my brother, Homer. He was so happy that he had a baby brother. I was told later that he was telling everyone that he met, about me . . . . that was OK at the time, but as I grew older, so did he, and before you knew it, he was more interested in football and "GIRLS", than in me. So, I took a backseat. Homer was 15 years old at the time.

Mother and Dad had a grocery store and were busy selling things like "buttereen" (today it is named margarine). There was a shortage of butter during the war; thus, this new product was introduced. Dad had a horse and wagon and the horse's name was "Daisy". Dad traveled around with the wagon, delivering grocery products. Things like sugar, cocoa, coffee, flour and the likes came packaged in wooden barrels and people would come into the store and buy these products by the pound.

Of course, the war I am speaking of was World War I. My three uncles, Harry, Walter and Russell were drafted into the Army during that time. I don't know much about those times, but I'm sure they were much the same as the days of World War II.

During this time, (1922) prices were as follows: roast of pork—14 cents per pound; a new Ford sedan went for $645.00.

My parents got an idea one day about buying a house and so they purchased a nice brick half double in Wilson Borough at 2127 Hay Street. Here I was, a little tyke, moving into a brand new home, and I was only six months old. Boy, how lucky can you get. My brother had the problem of going to school at Easton High and had to walk to 12th and Northampton Street each day—about 20 blocks. This being his senior year made it most important that he continue there.

My parents always had someone living at our house. If it was not my Aunt Marie, or Grandmother Litsinger, it was a star boarder. Mother was an excellent cook and always managed to invite somebody in for dinner. The dining room was used often and at times I didn't know whether the people who were living with us, were friends or family. Those were special days with many activities (depending on how you looked at it).

The Great Depression

    This was the time when the "The Great Depression" hit the country and threw a curve into everyone's lives . . . . People lost money in the stock market, banks went broke, men lost jobs and were out of work for a long time. My Dad was no exception. He kept his job, fortunately, but his wages were cut down to a bare minimum. He went from earning $70.00 per week to $15.00 per week. Well, you know what that did to the house buying in our family . . . . Mother and Dad "lost" the home to the bank and ended up paying the bank "rent". What a shame, after about seven years of payments to have to give it up and pay to live there. This must have been a low blow to my parents.
    Typical prices at this time were something like this: a Willy's sedan $318, Car Battery $7.95, Coffee 25 cents per pound and you could buy a Console Radio (floor model) for $132.00.
    During the time of depression, many a man came walking down the street selling things, such as umbrellas or brushes. It was a tough life because so many people were without money, or places to live, and food on their tables. There was no money available anywhere. My Dad used to go out on his route for the company and tried to collect on bills that were owed. I would go with him during the summer sometimes and he would return to the car saying, "These people don't have any money and can't pay, he isn't working". Fortunately for us we were able to get along, but barely. Mother used to take in sewing for many a woman, and she was good at it. I always got chased out of the living room while she fitted a dress on someone. I can still hear that "ole Singer" Sewing Machine going like mad and often those hours extended into the early morning.

We had a piano in our living room and the Litsinger gang was always there playing and singing. There were a lot of good voices in the family. Aunt Marie could play, so could my Cousin Merle and Uncle George would always sit down and play his own composition that he named "Umpty, Umpty". Everyone would laugh and get a big kick out of his actions. Family was very important in those days and they stuck together, even if they had a fight now and then. It had to be that way, because there were twelve kids in my father's family and I guess they got lonely for each other. Of course, there is another reason for these gatherings, there was no TV in those days and we had to make our own fun and enjoyment.

I'm afraid that families don't get together like that anymore. At least as of this writing the family does not have time for each other, or for some strange reason they just don't get along. It is a sad thing to talk about, because they are the ones who are missing the good times. The TV and the Computer control our society these days. Electronics are great, but they have taken away the fun that we made for ourselves—we were creative and grew up that way.

We lived a pretty simple life. Every once in a while we would all go to the movies; they were special. Mother was star struck. She liked anything that made her feel rich, for example, she was infatuated with the Royal Family in England and enjoyed anything pertaining to their life style . . . the elegance of it, as it were

The movies did the same thing to her . . . I don't mean that she spent much of her time going to the movies or reading movie magazines . . . but she again was spellbound by the glitter of it all. And in addition to that, she was great for reading mystery books . . . the scarier the better. She was a great gal, always doing for someone else.

I started taking piano lessons back around 1935, somewhere around my 12th birthday. A widowed lady named Mrs. Jones was teaching other kids in our block, trying to earn some money for herself. I heard these kids in the neighborhood playing the piano; I mean there were maybe six of them scattered around. They all were Mrs. Jones' students, so I told Mother that I wanted to learn to play. She welcomed my decision and a "star" was born. After some time, I was given a piano solo named, "Rustic Dance". I fell in love with it. I played it and played it and played it. Mother got so sick of hearing it that she took the sheet music away from me. One day she was out in the kitchen baking and she heard the strains of an old familiar tune . . . "Rustic Dance". She came into the living room where "guess who" was seated at the piano playing her favorite song. She laughed about it and I kept playing that "same ole tune".

The piano lesson phase gradually took over Mother's life and she decided to take lessons also. She contacted my cousin Merle and asked if she would teach her to play. I believe she took about ten lessons, which was her entertainment for a long time. It was rather funny to watch as she played, looking through her bifocals, playing several chords, again looking through her bifocals and playing more of the piece of music. She preferred church hymns, because her church life was very important to her. She loved her Lord and said so, many times. It sustained her through all her life time.

I often think of the tough life that my Mother had. Her father, Adam Fehr, was killed in Chapman's Quarry at the age of about 36. I'm told that he was standing off to the side while a big crane was lifting a huge slab of slate. The slate dropped a large chunk, which flew through the air and hit him, knocking him into the hole. My grandmother, Augusta, mother's sister Aunt Neely and Clara were living in a company owned house at the time and had to move out. The Company in those days, treated their employees like that. Unless you had a son in the family and could put him to work in place of the deceased, you had to move out . . . . "everything"!!

Therefore, they left and went to Easton, acquiring employment at St. John's Luthern parsonage on Ferry Street. Their duties were that of a maid and housekeeper. I am not quite sure whether Aunt Neely worked with them; she was the older sister. Mother was ten years old and had to drop out of school because of this. This was just the start of some sorrows for her.

During the early years of my life, my parents had acquired several friends, of which were a man and his daughter who had owned a jewelry and clock shop in the city. It was a pleasure to go and visit them occasionally and especially for me because they had retired several years before and as a result had brought many artifacts of their business to their home. Their home was filled with clocks of many kinds. The clocks that caught my attention time and time again were the Grandfather type. They were fascinating and continued to catch my attention at each hour strike. Their home was filled with all sort of "dings", "bongs" and the like at each hour strike. I enjoyed this time and looked forward to it each time that we visited them.

Later in this writing you will be able to see that as an adult I had not gotten over this fascination and proceeded to satisfy this attraction in my life. I just loved clocks, especially the great ones.

Getting back to the Depression Days, we found our clothes coming as hand-me-downs and homemade things. Fortunately, for our family, Mother was a very good tailor. My Dad contacted someone from the coal regions that owned a truck and arranged to take orders for "coal". The driver would take the orders from my father, load up his truck and make deliveries around the area. People were trying to save as much money as they could because they did not have much to begin with. Men would stand in line to get loaves of bread or soup that was given to them in a container that they supplied from home . . . and take it home to the family. Things were really desperate in those days. Banks went belly up and many men committed suicide. It was really tough living from day to day.

Those times that I am speaking of were in the early 30's, because after the depression hit, it left everyone with no job, no money, no home in many cases and "no—a-lot-of-things" . . . . with one exception, everyone had friends. Friends who had gone through the same situations and understood the problems. People were destitute and sought places of employment. Everyone had to make do with what they had. American ingenuity took over and people overcame the obstacles.

Franklin Roosevelt was elected president of the U.S. and took over at a very crucial time in the country's history. My mother and father got along on a little for a long time and were able to pull through the depression with a whole lot of effort. I never wanted for anything, nor do I remember having to go hungry or without clothing. I was cold sometimes because our bedrooms, upstairs, were not directly heated. The windows would freeze over during the night so much that you could not see out of them. Our furnace was coal fired and was pipeless. The register was in the center of the floor between the dining and living rooms. During the very deep winter, the section of the furnace in the basement would turn red with heat. I spent many a day dressing and getting ready for school at that spot . . . . it felt so good. Mother was able to put a pot of something really tasty on the inside ledge of the firebox downstairs and thus save on the use of gas to cook the meal. I remember many times when we had pork and sauerkraut or vegetable soup. It didn't matter what it was . . . I ate it and was thankful for it.

Our basement was never finished off like the homes of today. The furnace was placed on a cement base and the coal bin had a cement floor. The rest of the floor was dirt and required several long boards to walk on . . . . especially when there was water from the rains and melting snow. The room in the back of the basement was enclosed and contained shelves with a great amount of delicious canned goods that were prepared by Mother. Women did a great deal of canning in those days, for many reasons . . . to save on expenses and if lucky enough to have a garden, could save even more. Mother and the neighbor ladies would sit out on their front porches and talk while peeling apples or snapping beans.

When summer arrived I always looked forward to the homemade root beer . . . . It was so darn good and on a hot day it tasted extra special. The iceman was very busy during the summer months. As he drove down the street the kids would hitch a ride on the back of the truck or wagon, grab a large piece of ice and wet down their mouths with it.

We had another person that arrived when the weather changed in the spring and early summer . . . the "Rag Man." He drove a horse and wagon loaded with all kinds of junk. He would collect anything that you wanted to get rid of, or sell you anything that he had on the wagon. He used to come down the street yelling at the top of his voice, "Ay-yi! Ay-yi! Any rags today!"

Another person that arrived at that time, walked throughout the neighborhood carrying umbrellas . . . . "The Umbrella Man." His occupation, selling and repairing umbrellas. He may have been a very good mechanic at one time, but because of the depression, lost his job and resorted to this kind of livelihood so he could eat every day. Everyone in existence in those days was affected by the world conditions and had to make the most of it . . . . Yankee ingenuity took over.

At this time, 1940, the life expectancy was 62.9 years; radar was invented, the Dow Jones Average was 134. The average income was $1,725.00 per year. A new house was priced at $3925.00; a new car $850.00; a loaf of bread 8 cents; a gallon of gas 11 cents and a gallon of milk cost 51 cents.

In the meantime, I was getting ready for graduation from Wilson High School. My parents had sacrificed to give me things that I needed, including food, clothing and a few necessary items that were needed in order to finish school, such as a new outfit for the Senior Prom. My friend, Jack Seip, had a mother who didn't want him to go without anything, although she had trouble making finances do. She got him a new sport coat and new trousers .... my mother said, "Well, if he can have them, you are not going to go without". So, I too, was outfitted with a brand new outfit .... I remember it well .... a really nice green tweed sport coat and a fine pair of cream-colored trousers. Boy did I feel like I was somebody. I took a gal named Betty Kickline to the prom, corsage and all and we both had a great time. I never did learn to dance very well, but we filled our dance card rather quickly.

The new U.S. president, Franklin Roosevelt, took over in Washington and started the "New Deal" which was supposed to put bread and butter on the table again. People everywhere were just getting back to normal after Roosevelt's election when along came a real nut in Europe, named Adolf Hitler and he really started to mess things up .... the whole world would never forget this man. He disrupted so many lives, countries and peoples, that the history books would take many pages to tell of him.

Meanwhile, we were scheduled for Mid-Term Exams at school and I was right in the mist of them. One day, my Father experienced a heart attack, which disrupted the whole family. Being the forceful man that he was, he decided to go to work two days later. Several days went by and he experienced another attack. He treated this one the same way, waiting two days before going back to work. Again, he did the same thing, waiting for two days. One has to understand that coming out of a depression like he had, he was to conscientious for the good of himself. As a result, he experienced the third attack and passed away on January 25, 1940. The medical world didn't know much about heart attacks at that time and the doctor informed my Mother that men would be dropping from them very often in the future. How true his statement was.

That fateful day has stayed in my memory all these years and Mother had to go through another terrible time in her life .... she was a real trooper. That day, I was called from my bedroom to help to pick my Daddy up. I shall never forget it. He didn't take good care of himself physically, smoked like a chimney and loved to eat meat .... fat included. But with it all, Mother and I survived.

Graduation came and I managed to get through that, in the largest graduating class in the history of Wilson High School .... a big crop of 141. I was only seventeen years old at the time and my mother was receiving assistance from social security to help support me until I turned eighteen. Because of this, I had to find a job or go back to school for a post-graduate course. I chose the latter rather quickly. I attended Wilson High again in September and while there, I met the girl of my dreams . . . . Betty Ida Clewell. She sent me spinning almost immediately, although I had a degree of difficulty going with her because of her age . . . . she was just a freshman.

Soon after meeting Betty, the school called me into the office and said that they had a job for me. I immediately started working for an office supply house in downtown Easton on Bank Street under the name of Heymann's Office Supplies. This turned out to be a real experience and another chapter in my life history. As I look back on it and the way Mr. Heymann showed his authority was, in his mind, Big Time. He looked up at me from his desk and proceeded to read the riot act about how important my job was and that he wanted me to know that. I was hired to be trained to become a typewriter repairman, eh, excuse me, ahem! A typewriter engineer. It never happened. In addition, my duties included dusting and stocking the shelves in the store and delivering packages AND repairing typewriters. Delivering these things was another subject.

I was given money for bus fare and in so doing I would purchase a weekly pass. This offered me a chance to save a little bit each time, you see my salary was $12.00 per week . . . . I learned to be very saving during the depression and that hadn't changed. To go on with my delivery system . . . . I had to load up with (on a given day) a typewriter, several packages, such as reams of paper or other office supplies that took up all the arms I had and get on the bus while being transported out to Treadwell, Taylor Wharton, the Silk Mills on North 13th Street or maybe Wilson High School. It could become a circus and did on days when it rained and I maneuvered an umbrella in addition to everything else.

There were very good days, too . . . . those that allowed me to be at Wilson High School just as my girl friend, Betty, was leaving to go home . . . . so I would walk her home and I want you to notice that I never got back to the office late. Now that's planning. Ah yes, there are ways.

While working at Heymann's, I was responsible for taking the parcel post packages to the post office each day and it was during one of those times that I started looking for another job. I applied at Alpha Portland Cement Company, Metropolitan Edison Company and an application for a job in Washington, D.C. in Civil Service with the Government. I eventually took the job in Civil Service and left for Washington, D.C. soon after that.

Men and women were working in the factories and producing such things as automobiles . . . . people had money to purchase them. Washington was spinning with energy and activities.

Well, don't you know, along came World War II and changed everyone's lives. This time, it hurt in a different way and it lasted for a while. Industries had to retool in order to make the weapons of war. The wheels started turning, people were hired, a Bond Drive was started and the U.S.A. was back in business again.

While I was working in Washington, one week—days, next week—nights, I roomed at a home across town. It took me 45 minutes traveling time on the trolley to get to work. I was working for the War Department, Distribution Section, compiling Tables of Organization and other important forms that were eventually sent to the various Army units across the country and world. I eventually caught up to forms like that after entering the army several years later. But before those things happened, I had decided that I would need to resign my position in Washington and return to Easton and my mother. It was difficult for her and rather troublesome for me. I returned home by train every other weekend with funds for her to meet her expenses. By doing these things, I was able to get employment in Easton at several different places and finally ended up at The Taylor-Wharton Company.

After applying at Taylor-Wharton, I got a job in the Order Department. My expertise with the typewriter followed me wherever I traveled and it was responsible for my success later on in life. My job consisted of taking dictation (which I couldn't read), typing out order forms from the big companies ordering track work for the trolley and train lines. Also the Navy (which was now engaged in war) ordered gas cylinders by the thousands. These were used to handle gases of various sorts (oxygen, carbon dioxide, helium, etc.).

Uncle Sam Sends Greetings

I had worked at Taylor-Wharton about 2 years when I received a letter from the War Department, inviting me to take a physical and to look into making the military my life's work . . . . remember . . . . "Greetings" was the very cheeriest invitation for anyone of the age that Uncle Sam considered correct.

I passed my physicals. Many of my friends were already in the military branches. I went downtown to the Central Railroad Station (this has since burned down) and "All A-Board" to parts unknown. I was shipped to California. What an opportunity to see the country . . . . it took about 2 or 3 days to get there, but "there I did git". I arrived on a late Saturday evening in Camp Haan with no time to look around or get acquainted. I was assigned a bunk, foot locker, etc. and learned how to make a bed in a hurry, went to sleep, woke up Sunday morning with dew on the vented window above my bunk. From there on things went down hill for a while. It took all I could do to learn the ways, the Army ways, with everything "olive drab" color and only one right way to do things. I even approached my Commander about shipping back East, but he talked me out of it rather quickly.

Army life became "the way" and you did what you were told, or else. I served on KP and stood guard duty, went on various hikes, especially on a qualifying hike of 25 miles. I went to the firing range and qualified with the M-1, Sub-Machine Gun, Carbine, 30-caliber and 50-caliber Machine Guns. I camped out, in, over, up, down and got plenty dirty and tired. I was awarded various metals and one that I was proud of was the Sharp-Shooter metal, the middle of three that were awarded. Our most interesting experiences were always when we went to Camp Irwin out in the Mohave Desert for 6 weeks at a time. It was very hot during the day, very dry and very cold at night. We even were taken to Death Valley for a week-end, arriving dusty and dirty, but the place was most interesting, since it had been and still is a "Resort Area for the Rich & Famous".

I forgot to mention that I was assigned to the 834th AAA Battalion which was a unit assigned to the 10th Army later on. We had 40mm Antiaircraft Guns, many, many trucks and other vehicles. Originally we were considered part of the Coastal Artillery. In those days no one knew if the Japanese intended to attack California and as we look back on that time, we know now that they surely could have done that very thing. They had lobbed artillery into California at the very beginning; not many but they tried it and got away with it. Our nation was being attacked from East to West, but our Navy took care of things in their own great way.

Camp Cooke

We finished basic training for 6 weeks and then went to advanced training for 6 weeks. When we finished the training we were scheduled to join an infantry unit in Europe, but a change came through and we didn't go anywhere. Our unit was changed. We became a "Self-Propelled" Battalion. We had to change our Table of Organization (T/O) completely. We got rid of all of our 40mm Antiaircraft weapons and acquired a very large number of "Half-Tracks" mounted with "Quad-50mm Machine Guns" and a "Tri-mount of twin-50mm machine Guns" with a 37mm anti-aircraft gun in the center. We were being readied for Anti-Aircraft Support against low flying aircraft. Later on, the Army found better use for our half-tracks . . . ground assault. We were at Camp Cooke, California at this time.

Then came a drastic change. Camp Cooke was just a memory, along with Area 15—Camp Haan, Camp Irwin and the East Range, Fort Rosencrans, Camp Dunlap and California with all its breathtaking beauty that seemed to draw one to it. It was a long drag, a long training program and a good bit of fun in the states. Time had passed on its endless way and our allotted share of it was gone. Now we were headed for the Port of Embarkation.

We left Camp Cooke, sometime after I returned from my last furlough. Hopped a train there at the camp, and were on our way up the coast line to Vancouver, Washington.

We had loads of fun, and as we traveled north we could notice the change in climate and terrain. We passed Mt. Hood. It was beautiful as could be, covered from head to shoulders with snow. The wind tucked the downey flakes into each nook and cranny.

Our train pulled into Vancouver Barracks, Vancouver, on a cold rainy day. We got off the train, slung our duffel bags on our shoulders, and took off for the trucks. The camp band played as we loaded our equipment and marched up to the top of the camp to our new barracks. There we were situated among the pines; I could picture the place in the summer time even as I breathed the clear air, the beauty of a pictured summer here surrounded me.

Then began the routine of getting set for overseas duty. We had showdown inspections, rifle inspections, medical inspections, inocculations and still more inspections. Plus training films, lectures, and all of the usual routine; classes on the Japanese, aircraft recognition, and many others.

The chow was great and the best I had eaten since being in the service, and a guy doesn't have to be a good judge of cooking to know that Army chow is out of this world—way out.

We got our new combat boots. Everyone was limping this way and that trying to break them in. we soaked them in saddle soap and dubin until we thought they were soft enough to take a nap on, but they cut the ankle bones just the same; however, the day came when they were the most comfortable thing that ever had been on our feet.

There were passes, after a few days of waiting, until our shots took effect. We enjoyed them tremendously, the passes, I mean, going into Vancouver, and Portland, Oregon. What a town, women running all over; but they didn't affect me, affect me, affect me.

Finally the day came when we were all packed and were to leave. We got up in the early morning, cleaned out the barracks, stacked the bunks in an orderly manner, and marched down to the trucks. Off we went to the docks. When we boarded the ship, we had our steel helmets on with our rifles slung on one shoulder and our duffel bag on the other. We wondered whether we could make it up the gangplank. The Red Cross workers were there passing out doughnuts and coffee. And as we stood around, the thought came to mind of the new life that lie ahead of us. And we wondered if our training was going to help—we surely hoped it would. "Let's go men", and up the gangplank we went, down to the berthing compartments, grabbed a bunk (in an orderly fashion, oh yeah!), and laid down until everyone was aboard.

Hawaii Bound

At this point in time I must tell you that Hawaii, as we know it today, had not become a state and this writing addresses much of interest pertaining to the "Islands", as they were during the war years while the United States was engaged in this great conflict.

Our ship, "The Sea Partridge", got under way, down the Columbia River and out to sea. We stood on deck, along the rails from the bow to the fantail and waved to the many people we saw on the shore. Soon we hit the choppy waters of the bay, and not long after that, the ocean waves. We had life boat drills and abandon ship drills all the way over and we did our best to get up the gangway as fast as possible, so that we wouldn't have to do it all over again.

Well, it was that way all the time while on board. Some of the guys, in fact, many of the guys, were sick. The ship had been hit (or so we were told) by a bomb in the forward compartment several months before, while carrying Marines on an invasion, and she now was out of line. We dipped and turned with every wave. Even a fish would get seasick from that. I was sick one of the days out of the seven that we were afloat; but I kept my meals down like an old salt and felt much better because I did. Others became friends with the railing and thereafter were there all of the time feeding the fish.

It was a beautiful trip all the way over, and we didn't encounter a bit of trouble from the Japs at all. One storm that we hit was rather bad, but it could have been worse, and we came through it more weathered than before.

Finally "land ho" was sounded, and there was "Diamond Head", the big mountain on Oahu. Dreaming of Hawaiian breezes and grass skirts as we were, certainly increased the beauty on that island at the time; but looking at land from several miles out, is a lot different than the actual close-ups. We came into the harbor, and just like a bunch of kids, were anxious to see everything we could. Several of the guys that were with us at that time, were stationed on Oahu during the Pearl Harbor attack, and they pointed out all the places of interest.

We docked, and began unloading and convoying up to our staging area. Everyone was hustling and scurrying about. We found it to be much like the good ole U.S.A. Our eyes were wide and roving, our minds awake; for this was a place of history. Pearl Harbor was stretched out before us.

Hawaii, we thought, would be different, we had pictures of it being like the books. Government workers, shipyards, harbors, laborers, servicemen and women, and Orientals were all over the place doing their bit for the war effort.

After a long dusty ride, we entered our area, overlooking Pearl Harbor. It was nice and cool there at night, and warm during the day. We drilled, and did everything just as though we were back in the states. We stayed there long enough to pick up our new vehicles. That is when I got my new Jeep, and was it great. Nicely painted, everything new; and it ran like a top . . . . why, this was my very first new car.

A day later we moved to a section of Schofield Barracks, named the East Range. We set up in little huts or houses, which at one time were used by Japanese families. After Pearl Harbor these families were rounded up and put in this camp—it was all fenced in, and used as an internment camp. We took over from there on, cleaning out the huts, and making life as easy as we possibly could.

We ordered new equipment and issued it to the men. And by the time we left the place, we were just about the best outfitted and equipped troops on the island. I'm sure of that, for our duffel bags were near the bursting point.

Chow was rough over there, and each morning we would hop in the Jeep, and buzz down the road to the town of Wahiawa to get a cup of coffee and fried eggs.

The people were friendly enough, but they always turned away from us whenever possible. There were some, however, who talked now and then, but very few. Perhaps we had not gotten used to the oriental way of living, and the oriental life, for they seemed strange to us for a long time. When the girls started to look pretty to us, and the peoples' skin started turning white, we always smiled.

Each day was busier than the first, and we were glad to hit the sack each night. We looked forward to the volley ball games every evening, and playing football, or even baseball, whenever we could find time.

There were many times when we had to work way into the wee hours of the morning, getting out the necessary work that had to be done before our shipping orders came in.

It rained in our area nearly every day. Just behind us, was a range of mountains, with the ocean on the other side. Therefore, the clouds had quite a bit of fun, picking up the water on one side and dropping it on us.

Sundays, if we were lucky, we had an off day; in the morning, we had church services and in the afternoon we hopped on a truck and went swimming at Soldiers Beach, or at the pool at Schofield Barracks.

Schofield Barracks took a beating when the Japs hit Pearl Harbor. The barracks are still full of bullet holes which the strafing planes of the Nips left as their marker.

Swimming was a wonderful thing off the beaches of this beautiful island. The waters round about are just as blue and clear as the sky itself. We used to dive way below the surface of the water, using diving masks, and had fun watching small octopi and fish of all colors. During our training period while there, we had to go swimming with all our clothes on, as a precautionary measure to see if we could actually swim with added weight—just in case. The sun always seemed to be shining, and each day there was a new layer of brown on our backs.

I know everyone has heard or read about Waikiki Beach in the Hawaiian Islands. When passes were available, we always hitched a ride into Honolulu and from there got a bus to Waikiki.

The beach was beautiful, the sun hot and the water cool and refreshing. We rented surfboards and paddled out to the breakers. Then the job began—trying to stand on the board while it scooted along on the crest of the whitecaps. It was easy to sit or lay on the board; but when two of us used a board there was always the fun and delightful pleasure in turning the board over and spilling the other guy.

After an afternoon of swimming, we spent our time in a likely looking restaurant, munching on a supposedly tender steak. At least it tasted like one, and that was the main thing.

There was a curfew at 11:00 PM each night, and we had to be off the streets at that time. We usually stayed at the Holiday House in Honolulu, which was run by G.I.'s. There were several large buildings which had sleeping accommodations, and they were all centered around a large and beautiful lawn. At night it was nice to sit there in the quiet and dream of the many things that seem to pass through a soldiers mind.

Hawaii had become very American in the time that it had been under our care. The Island of Oahu is very beautiful in every respect. The coconut palms wave their fingers at the sky, clouds never seem to darken the island, and the climate is ideal. All in all, we enjoyed our short stay there very much, and will always recall Hawaii and its beauty.

The day of shipment finally came; passes ceased to exist as far as we were concerned. We worked day and night, with a shift for each eight hours taking over. We crated everything we possibly could. We loaded on three ships. One of them was loaded down to the gunwales with ammunition of all types. The rifles started to look more like a friend than an enemy. The bayonets were sharpened, and drills were held for all. We fired Carbines, Rifles and Tommy Guns, just to get set for—anything, we didn't know what; but the Brass surely did.

Then one morning—very early—we climbed on the trucks, fully packed, and headed for the docks. It was a typical Army day, only the Navy was in on this one, too; for after leaving so early, we ended up by sitting around on the docks for a full half day, until time to board the ship. The word was passed down the line, and we started to move toward our ship. This was the beginning.

WE SAIL INTO . . . . ?

On the afternoon of March 27, 1945, we boarded the "U.S.S. Audubon". It was an APA (Assult Personnel Attack Ship). A big blue baby, filled with landing craft, rafts and loaded down with equipment and food for a long voyage.

We struggled on board with our new equipment, loaded down to the gills, as it were. We had received two canteens, a jungle kit, mosquito bars, mosquito gloves, head nets, mosquito repellant, atabrine tablets, waterproof matchboxes, first aid packets, all new clothing of a dark green color for camouflage and many other things that were to prove useful in the future.

After we got settled, finished looking around the ship, and nosing here and there, we began rounding out each day with reading, eating and writing letters. We had movies on board ship, as long as we were in port someplace. We got acquainted with the "swabbies" (a name given to the sailors), and knew where this and that guy lived in the states. We had air raid drills, and the gun crews fired now and then to keep in practice. (All of this time we came across in convoys of about twenty or more ships).

During our period on the water, which later turned out to be a month—we heard of the news of President Roosevelt's death. It came as a blow to all of us, and everyone was very much surprised, for he had done so much for the country. We realized that there had to be a very good man somewhere to take his place.

Then Easter came in all its splendor and the grand glory of Our Lord and Saviour was ever present. Time passed slowly it seemed, and each Sunday came upon us rather unexpectedly, but each was more beautiful than the first. Perhaps our heading for combat had something to do with making the familiar things before our eyes become more real than they had been before.

We stopped enroute to our destination for a breather at Antiwetok in the Marshall Islands. The trip from Oahu, Hawaii could never be replaced, and beauty picked from each spacious moment will always be remembered.

This island in the Marshalls stands as one of the permanent monuments for the Marines who gave their lives in the fight for freedom against the Japanese. It was hot and the lagoon was choppy.

We went swimming off Perry Island and almost could forget the war and our parts in it. We stood in line until we were able to buy a case of warm coke or beer.

Mail came through and followed us wherever we went; it became a living thing in our lives; and the greatest morale builder of them all. We looked for it day after day.

We got underway once again, still in the same general direction. Everyone seemed tight with anxiety, wanting to know more about the job in the near future. We all had one desire—to get this thing over with—and go back to our homes, but we weren't the first, nor the last to have those thoughts.

Our ship plunged her bow proudly forward into each blue wave, turned white by the moving hand of the wind. The Pacific, being true to form, acted like a chameleon, changing from a deep, placid blue, to an emerald green. Now and then a school of silvery blue flying fish winged across in front of us. A porpoise could be seen running along with us, breaking the surface at intervals. High overhead the billowy white clouds nosed through the blue, like majestic watchdogs of the sky.

Sunday always was a quiet day on board, because during the services all ships' work ceased, and everyone was reverent. Many a time it rained during our services, but we sat through it all on the hatch cover. Out there rain comes and goes quickly. The sun had us completely dry by the time the service closed.

The nights were dark and quiet. Above the throbbing noise of the engines could be heard the rolling, tossing sea beneath us; with whitecaps very prominent. The ocean seemed different at times, more different than before—it was a dark, deep thing; which would toss us about, were a storm to break through. The skies were bleak and gray; making forms throughout the vastness of the skies. Our ship rode well, now up, now down, just as the swells.

The air was warm and stifling. Sleep was difficult; eating more so. Sweat poured forth and water took its place. We all wished for better things, but it was just a wish. One day was just the same as others had been; we were merely sailing along, to what, we knew not. The Navy crews kept up a vigilant watch for the enemy, and now and then they traced a handsome, destructive pattern in the sky while shooting down towed targets.

Our ship pulled into the Caroline Islands. They weren't as barren as the Marshalls, for more vegetation could be seen growing on them. Still the heat was terrific. We weren't allowed on shore while there. We stayed for nearly five days, oiling up, watering up and waiting for further orders to go on. We enjoyed movies each night. It rained during shows; but we sat there and got soaked, just as we did back in Oahu.

Then the day came when we got underway once more, and the screws turned in symphonic rhythm, closing the miles between us and our destination. We knew where it was and it looked like hot stuff from there on. They informed us over the ships loudspeaker system. When told of our destination, some cheered, some, no doubt, felt glum and others were expressionless; but at least one thing was certain—the long voyage would be over; and when approached from a certain angle, it was closer home—one way or another.

Destination .... Okinawa

Under cover of an intense naval bombardment, the XXIV Army Corps and the III Marine Corps established beachheads on the west coast of long, narrow Okinawa on 1 April 1945. Aided by a realistic feint toward the thickly populated southern tip of the island, our forces met little resistance in the landing and in consolidating positions ashore. After driving across the island, the Marines swung northward against light to moderate opposition; the Army turned south toward Naha, principal city of the island, where it was confronted by the main Japanese force elaborately entrenched.

After moping-up all of the northern part of the island, the Marines took over a sector in the south to throw their weight into the drive for Naha. Progress continued slow against the bitterest sort of opposition but by the middle of June, our troops had broken through the heavily fortified Naha and Shuri defense lines and had compressed the Japanese into two pockets on southern Okinawa.

The ferocity of the ground fighting was matched by frequent Japanese air assaults on our shipping in the Okinawa area. By the middle of June, 33 U.S. ships had been sunk and 45 damaged, principally by aerial attacks.

By mid-June, the Japanese had lost twenty percent of their total combat aircraft strength in the battle for Okinawa; in all, 3,400 Japanese planes were shot down over the Ryukyus and Kyushu and 800 more were destroyed on the ground. During the same period our losses totaled more than a thousand aircraft. By the end of June we had suffered 39,000 casualties in the Okinawa campaign, which included losses of over 10,000 among naval personnel of the supporting fleet.

By the same date, 109,629 Japanese had been killed and 7,871 taken prisoner.

The news came through that the 10th Army had invaded Okinawa on April 1, 1945 (April Fools Day—for the Japanese). We were part of that huge 10th Army and very proud of it. Things didn't look so good there for a while, and we wondered whether we would have to go up on the beaches shooting or not. Each day we were closer, going in a zig-zag course all the way.

The gunners were on watch on a 24-hour basis. We had no trouble with the Jap planes, but we were followed by submarines all the way. I don't know whether we got any or not. Depth charges were dropped many times by our escorts and once a Horn mine was blown up by one of the escorts. It no doubt had broken loose from its moorings and started a free-for-all-floating-jamboree around in the Pacific.

At night it was nice to stand on deck and watch the waters churning beneath the bow of our ship. At dusk, all smoking on deck was stopped, all lights were put out, and all hatches were blacked out. Guards were established all night long on deck, and fire watchers had their duties to perform throughout the night. Water was turned on at certain hours, so that we had to crowd in and shave, or shower with the next guys' elbow in your ribs all of the time.

Chow was announced over the ships' loudspeaker system, as was everything else. Three times a day, we heard the words, "Now Hear This, Now Hear This—All men holding mess tickets 1 to 700 fall in line for chow on the starboard side of the boat deck." The navy has a system all its own.

We Land On Purple Beach

The afternoon of April 25th we pulled up to the island of Okinawa. Planes of the Navy flew over us, keeping on the lookout for everything imaginable. We saw a mighty aramada of ships: hospital ships, vessels and landing craft, swirling about; carrying men, supplies, equipment, food and others coming from shore with the wounded.

The light ship stood out above all others, blinking, signaling in its own special way, telling this one and that one to stay out or to come in and dock. It brought to mind a mother cluck calling her brood.

In the distance we could see the island with its growth of trees, flowers and bushes. All was quiet on the Northern end of the island. The dust that was raised by hundreds of rolling wheels told a story all its own.

The Southern end was different. There was a dense, foglike atmosphere above it, yet we knew it was smoke; smoke from hellish explosions and fire. The Navy battlewagons stood off shore and continuously pounded the enemy. Navy dive bombers kept constantly laying their eggs in the Jap positions and straffing the enemy troops. There was no air opposition whatsoever. How long the enemy could stand up under such punishment was beyond our imaginations, and although we didn't know, we didn't care, for the Navy looked mighty good at the time.

The long tiresome trip across the Pacific had come to a close. We were excited, for new things lie on shore, awaiting our coming.

We started our unloading operations, and transporting our supplies by landing craft and Higgins boats up to the temporary wharfs built by the engineers and CB's; and as the men went over the side to the landing craft below, I wondered when it would be till we did that very same thing in a harbor at home.

We were the last to leave the ship and as we sailed away, we said goodbye to the blue lady of the deep. The Officer of the Deck gave us a greeting and wished us luck.

The throbbing Higgins boat finally pulled into one of the long landing docks. Men and equipment were everywhere. The harbor was light as day. Here we were in combat and they had more lights than New York City. At that moment we experienced a new concern, the air raid sirens sounded and the harbor blacked out.

We loaded our duffel bags on a truck and took off for a bivouac area, somewhere just in back of the beach. Everywhere we looked, the CB's had bulldozers working, making roads, in and out with their loads of sand.

The trucks came to a stop and we piled out. What light we had was from the moon, which was slowly running behind the clouds. The stars were out, yet in the distance were those ever present rain clouds. It was 2 o'clock in the morning, and as we walked up into the fields, we could see the rest of our outfit laying on their blankets. We dug foxholes, then laid our ponchos and a blanket down for a bed—some bed. The dew started to settle on us.

It seemed like I had just closed my eyes, when the air raid sirens sounded. We crawled out of our holes, climbed into our (what did we think, we were on a camping trip!) fatigues, slapped on our helmets (each verb holds true in this case). The Navy was laying down a smoke screen, covering the harbor, hiding the many ships that lay at anchor. We waited, wearing our helmets, wishing for the ship once more and that broad expanse of water, but our fears were quelled, for the Japs didn't arrive—they were engaged over the sea. We slept the rest of the night peacefully (if you can call it that), with our weapons loaded and waiting. This was like a picnic, no Japs around us . . . . of course we were in support of those in the front lines. Our clothes stayed put from then on.

Day Two

Nearly twenty-four hours had passed since we made our landing on "Purple Beach". We had undergone many new experiences in that course of time and could be called veterans. Surely we were all afraid, but fear in combat is a natural thing, and if a man isn't afraid, there certainly is something wrong with him. That night of April 26th, 1945, had passed, but it will always be in my memory. We were lucky.

The sun brought us out from our nighttime nerve racking experiences and we stretched and grunted like the usual run of civilians do after a bad night. Soon fires were lighted, rations were being cooked and we were learning the rudiments of field soldering, instead of practicing as we did many months before. We gathered what water we could, and washed whenever possible, which wasn't very often. Our helmets became a wash basin with water for everything possible.

After chow we stacked our equipment, and set out as individuals and groups to scour the nearby countryside. Some of the guys caught goats that were roaming around and forgot the war for awhile to bring back childhood memories on the farms.

The Okinawan people are very sincere in their belief of burying their dead. We visited the tombs that they hold sacred. Many were blown open by shell fire during the beginning of the campaign and we found them very interesting. They are built into a hill side in a funny way and constructed so the evil spirits will slide down off the top and up into the air again (like a ski jump).

They take their dead and seal them in these tombs, leaving them there for 7 years. After the 7 years have passed, they come back, open the tomb and place the bones in large ceramic vases or urns. Those of the more aristocratic families were colored with green and blue glazes. We found out later that the Japs used these tombs many times as sniper positions.

As we made our advances we had to be careful of stepping on a huge number of dead Japanese. There were hands, arms, legs and heads sticking out of the earth at various points. The place smelled of "death" and we had taken charge of our bivouac area as though we were home in the states, digging slit trenches to spend the night. It didn't take long for the Japanese to change our minds in a hurry. They sent bombers over, looking to take out our ships in the harbor and yours truly on land. Everyone ran for a more protective location and ended in a pile-up at one of the burial spots that the Okinawians used for their dead.

Later in the day it rained, making life very miserable. By the time it stopped, mud was our biggest problem and we set our pup tents on a grassy knoll. Things dried out and everyone was glad of that. It grew dark fast and late that night we experienced another air raid. A few planes got through our defenses and headed for airfields and harbor. The sky was like day with the searchlights piercing the sky. A "Francis" came over, laid its eggs and zig-zagged through the pattern of aircraft fire. It was like a fourth of July and we certainly were not used to this new experience.

Our AA defense of the island was one of the most spectacular things that I have ever seen in connection with air operations. There was a circle of ships way out at sea all of the time, picking up planes with their radar equipment. They would radio in to the island, and the island would send up its planes for the inner defense. There was an outer defense of planes flying around the island the whole day. Then there was an inner defense, doing the very same thing. When we had an air alert, the planes either stayed on the ground or left the island, depending upon how many were needed and how many were ordered out. The AA took care of anything that got through, which wasn't very often. The Japs would leave Japan, hoping to do their best; but our planes took care of them. One week our planes had 750 or more kills to their credit, which is a good average. The Japs were noted for flying with our formations until day break, and then taking off as fast as they could for home. Every night thereafter it was the same thing all over again.

Not knowing the many sounds of warfare was one thing against us that first night and we nearly killed each other heading for a foxhole, however, we found the noise to be our own guns firing. The rolling, piercing sound of the larger guns took to the hills and was gone; while the sharp staccato of the smaller guns kept up a steady incessant chatter. Sleep was nearly impossible, for the Japs were busy all night long. We always were thankful for a moonlight night. It was easy to see any Jap that might be creeping around in the darkness; but it also aided the Jap bombers. They always picked a night when the moon was out and the sky covered, slightly, with streaks of clouds.

Our biggest fear thus far, was a Japanese 105 mm gun position (later nicknamed Pistol Pete), back in the hills at the southern end of the island. It was situated in a cave, and each night it would come out of the cave, fire a few rounds and go back in. Our artillery never could find its range. I didn't say never did; but never could at the time. It was zeroed in on Kadena Air Strip, just 500 yards in back of our bivouac area. Each night it shelled the air strip in back of us and The whistle of the shells could be heard as they passed over us. We used to lay there in our foxholes and count them and we would time the intervals between each round. We lucked out with this activity, always expecting the worst.

Our C, K and D rations were finally replaced with 10-in-1 rations, and the art of cooking inherited from good common sense, was brought forth. Bacon, cereal, peas, pork, beef, jelly and all sorts of things that tasted good after a long while of going without.

The Rainy Season

Our biggest problem came with the rainy season. It came down in torrents and left nothing but knee deep mud. Vehicles bogged down and the Engineers worked hard on the roads, only to have to build them up again. The mud was sticky and slippery, making travel very difficult. Typhoon season set in and one of those just missed the island on a single day.

When the rainy season came along, we had an awful time. Driving was the meanest kind of a job, and I became one of those mean drivers. The mud, and narrow roads taught me to drive, if nothing ever will. Getting stuck here and there, and putting it in four wheel drive, the granny gear, and the jeep would just walk out of that mud hole like nobodys business. The mud didn't help any when it became very evident that we must take off and go, for the snipers were having a picnic, even though they didn't make so many hits. Don't believe that yarn, however, about the Jap not being a good shot, just because he has bad eyes—its false.

The Japs didn't bother us as much with air raids anymore during this time of rain. Perhaps it was the low ceiling; but the full facts I do not know. I'm sure they had learned they must pay dearly to even get one plane through.

I saw the ambulances coming back from the front lines all during the campaign. Each little bump was an obstacle, and those drivers did a great job. Then the trucks carrying the dead would come back also. And there was always that odor about them. But after the first couple of times, you forgot such things, for it became a common occurrence.

We moved further south, not knowing what to expect. The enemy had been scattered in different directions and proved a very worthy opponent, with Banzi attacks and air cover; this being made possible because the Island of Okinawa is just off the coast of Japan. And in addition to this, the weatherman decided to dump a rainy season on us. We went days and weeks without a change of dry socks and shoes. The countryside was so muddy that the vehicles slid off the crown of the roads into the ditch. We had a miserable time trying to keep our weapons and equipment dry. Finally the rain left up and things started to dry out again. The time had come to move south once more. One night we got into a fire fight with who we didn't know, but it turned out to be the Engineers just across the road from us. Nobody was hurt, which we were thankful for, but what a night until that was over. Each outfit was sure that they had the enemy infiltrating into their lines.

We received word to move up to a new area. Our first mission was finished and now we had two new ones—protecting the Machinato Airstrip and the shore line several miles from Naha.

Our new area was nice and a very historical place on which to live. Kakaza Ridge, taken eleven times by the guys before keeping it. Nearby stood Chocolate Drop Hill, and Sugar Loaf where the boys drove the Japs back in one of the bloodiest battles of the campaign.

Kakaza Ridge was taken many, many times by both the Japs and the Yanks. There were still signs of a tough struggle—equipment scattered here and there; Jap bodies all over and Jap mines dangerously hidden. We had to bury the bodies, so the flies would go away and not be so bothersome to us.

We did some souvenir hunting in one of the villages just around the bend of the hill. We found a Jap sniper laying under the tree he sought as shelter while praying on our infantry as it advanced. He was caught in a hail of Tommy gun slugs from the waist up and not a pretty sight.

Some of the guys collected Jap rifles, bayonets, Samari swords, kamonias, dishes; things that were of no military value to the government.

Throughout the camp area were scattered caves, of all sizes and shapes winding through the hills and connecting to many entrances. By the sweat of their evil yellow bodies, they dug these out by hand, in a vain hope that they might someday live to see their achievement.

We pulled guard many a night with our hearts running wild in our chests, for each little movement kept us on the alert.

We were situated on this ridge overlooking a green fertile valley below. Rice paddies were laid out in systematic patterning. As the wind blew it took each strand of rice and bent it over so that it appeared to be praying. Shell holes and mortar holes zigzagged across the countryside. As my gaze met the furthermost hill, the sea came up to meet my view. It was a beautiful sight; the horizon lined with ships. The sun after a long day of crossing the heavens would go on its endless way, slowly ducking its yellow head behind a cluster of cumulus buildups. The affect was much the same as those at any other place in the world—with one exception—the Japs have put rays leading from the sun on their flags, and I often wondered what thought came into their minds that caused that. Now I know.

At eventide when the sun is setting or in the morning when it is rising, beautiful rays of red and orange pierce through the azure spaces and the Japanese flag is brought to mind immediately. No doubt, the Japs had those rays in mind when they named their homeland "The Land of the Rising Sun". I haven't ever seen those rays any other place in my travels, and they have to be seen to be appreciated.

Weeks passed and we built the area up until it looked more like home the whole day through. The Motor Pool was below us, a volleyball court on the ridge above us. A creek of cold fresh water ran into the rice paddies below, and each night we went down in the ravine to bath. The Okinawan people made places in the rock to bath and wash their clothes; now that they were gone, we put it to use. It's a picture when you think of it—"a bunch of nude guys bathing in this 'hole-in-the-wall'". The water brought back many memories of the Bushkill Creek at home and how we used to swim in it. All through the campaign we had to draw water from designated points where the Engineers purified it. The drums of water lie in the sun all day long, and many a times we wished for the coolness of fresh water to wet our throats. At eventide, after a long hot day, we longed for a cool shower, but again the sun had heated what we used.

The nights were beautiful and being that way made a guy dream. It made me homesick to sit and look out at sea, watching the sun go down and in back the moon coming up. Many a night I sat and watched the moon playing with the clouds, almost holding out a hand and saying, "Come along".

To look at the stars was as great a pleasure. All of this brought back memories of my boyhood when I used to lay on my back in the yard and watch the stars, wondering what held them up in the sky, and what made them wink at me. Each night there was a certain star that caught my eye—it twinkled just like—well, just like a star. Then my dreams became prayers and in the stillness of the night I talked with my Lord. It was good to know that He was with me, protecting and loving.

Now and then a flare bit into the darkness on a far Southern hill and as its light faded and went out, you would wonder how many Japs were creeping around out there and how many would never creep again.

A battery of artillery—Long Toms and 75's, always shattered the stillness. Flashes of light and the noise of shells piercing the sky as they point their noses into the Jap lines. Then quiet, as the night tries to become itself again.

Finally, a flashlight interrupted my dreams and I knew it was time for my shift of guard duty. Post #4 tonight—no one liked it and there I would be up on the hill among the pines. On a moonlight night it was perfect, but out here it could get mighty dark, and one could expect anything with the Japs still hiding in the caves around us.

Our Battalion was to protect artillery positions from attack from the air. All day and night we had the incessant hammering of Long Toms and 75's going on around us. One night Pistol Pete opened up and gave himself away. Our artillery was waiting for just that opening. They opened up with all that they had; from then on Pistol Pete was history in the campaign.

Everybody was rather trigger-happy, not having encountered any enemy activity at hand, but always on the alert for infiltration. The Japs were good at that, but the Marines had taken such good care of that maneuver, that they had them corralled at the southern part of the island and were engaged in one of the biggest and deadliest of battles in the Pacific. More than 49,000 perished on Okinawa.

In the meantime, back at the bivouac area, we posted guards for the night, with flares set up to trip in case of infiltration. The Okinawa people were a farming people and had horses and pigs that eventually got loose during the campaign. The horses were free to roam over the countryside. It is a wonder that they didn't get killed . . . . Maybe some did; but during this particular night, while on guard duty, the flares were tripped and the countryside lite up like daytime. One guy on guard duty started shooting into the dark just before the flare went up. There was a beautiful horse running loose and he remarked later, "Hey you guys, what would have happened if I had shot that horse, the hole that I would have had to dig to bury it . . . wow"! So, even in wartime, the American GI was able to look at the funny side.

We were troubled with snipers all during the campaign. Driving trucks and jeeps was no cinch when a sniper was liable to pop out at us. We were fired on several times, the bullets whizzing close over our heads, some of which tore through the sides of our vehicles. I came back with a jeep one day with bullet holes in the water can on the back and another time I came back with my spare tire gone flat because of a large piece of shrapnel embedded in it. I was fortunate.

The line batteries were busy on the beaches closer to the front than we were. The Japs attempted many times to get through our lines, and around into our midst, by the water route. So the batteries were kept on the alert, and they did their share of the work in that respect.

The job of Headquarters Battery was to supply the line batteries with food, clothing, ammunition and other necessities. The line batteries had a different situation, for they were closer to the line of fighting. They accounted for a number of snipers.

The 834th AAA, a Self-Propelled Antiaircraft Battalion, was ever alert to cover the battle from low-flying aircraft. Truth is, the Japanese aircraft didn't make much of an effort because they had been blown out of the skies, and being so close to their homeland, the Navy and Air Force kept them there, although the U.S. Navy lost many ships during that battle. We later located at Naha Air Field in the south and that became our permanent position until the war ended with the dropping of the 1st Atomic Bomb . . . it just devastated Hiroshima, a city in Japan.

The End Is Near

Shagushi Ridge, just across the ravine, will always hold its place in the annuals of history. Everywhere one goes on the island, he sees nothing but ridges and hills that spell battles. The trees, rocks and various caves were still black and shattered from the instruments of war.

All this time the guys were driving the Japs closer to the Southern tip of the island we were looking forward to the end of the campaign at any time.

General Buckner sent his surrender notice to the Jap commander, but it was sneered at, and no word was received. They chose the inevitable end, and they got it. From every corner in back of the lines the artillery laid it on thick; the infantry waited and finally everything was thrown in. We watched vehicles of all types, and trucks filled with replacements going to the front.

General Buckner was killed on May 26th while directing operations at the front. A Jap artillery shell found its mark and he knew no more.

We occupied Kakaza Ridge for a length of time and one day orders came for our movement up to Naha Airfield. We knew that our moving out would only make a better area for somebody else back along the operations area, and soon after, were to pass a handsome hill that was once a field of battle.

In moving south as we had, we accomplished one thing, if nothing else—the further south we were positioned, the more we knew that the Japs were being pushed back. We looked for the end of the campaign any day.

The War's End

And then it came—the end of the campaign and organized resistance. This was June 21, 1945. I figured that I was close to civilian life again . . . . but I figured wrong. The Army wasn't ready to release me; it had other things for me to do.

Cities and farms of Okinawa were laid low by bombs and shell fire as the infantry slowly advanced. The Engineers, looking for booby traps and mines, ransacked homes that used to be. The civilians left behind goats, cows, horses, chickens and pigs. We took full advantage, riding the horses until the government reclaimed them. We had roast pork for one meal and it was rather good. The chickens laid everyday and we anxiously waited for enough eggs to go around. The peeps grew fast and we got a kick out of them running around. They usually ended up in the mess hall looking for something to eat. One of the boys baked rolls and they were perfect enough to go under the name of Parker House.

Naha Airfield

We pulled up stakes, pulled down tents, packed and were soon on our way. Our trucks were busy carrying men and equipment once again. Being a self-propelled outfit made for easy transportation. Early that evening we arrived at our new area—Naha Airfield.

It was a semi-sandy portion on the far side of the airfield near the seawall. Covered with a grassy growth, and pine trees; it presented a picturesque effect in comparison to our old areas—no mud. At one end was a large hill, made up of one large cave used as a gun emplacement by the Nips. We sandbagged this in and used it as our C.P. later to become a haven of rest from "The Big Wind".

West of us was a village, torn and shattered, a mere ghost of a town. We found several wells just near the outskirts of it and put them to good use many times in the course of weeks, by bathing and doing our laundry in the water from them.

We set up our area, and in doing so, one of our bulldozers hit a Jap land mine, and threw the driver 20 feet or more. The dozer wasn't so bad, for the blade took the beating, and the driver, was just dazed. He was up and around a few days later.

We liked the new area very much, for it was near the ocean and we liked to swim, so each afternoon we walked just 100 yards out to the beach, and rumped in the blue waters.

We set up a theater, a large mess hall, battalion headquarters, officers row, our rows, a PX, a baseball diamond, and a volley ball court. Each day saw something new added to it, and it became the best home a man had since hitting the island.

The nights were cool, with the sea breezes coming in and hitting us. We slept under our mosquito bars, because of the swamps nearby, took our atabrine daily, and had every afternoon off. However, we were very busy every morning around 2 AM; for that seemed to be the only time that the Japs could come over to bomb the place. The siren would sound, and we would climb out of bed, helmets on and our rifles in our hands, and jump into our foxholes in our backyard. Then we would wait—sometimes for 15 minutes, other times for 2 hours. The next morning when we got up we looked like we could go back to bed.

The heat was terrific each afternoon. We got a new Colonel who knew what he was doing and was all for the men. So one morning at one of our formations, he spoke to us, and told us that work would begin at an earlier hour each morning, and we would stop work at noon. The rest of the day was spent in sack time, or playing ball, or swimming. Anything, just so we could have that time to ourselves. It sounds like it was the life—well, it was definitely, but others all over the island were doing exactly the same thing. To lay on a cot without being bothered by anyone during an afternoon, was great, in comparison with loading trucks with ammunition in knee-deep mud.

Several nights were spent in a foxhole watching Jap planes being shot out of the sky. I remember distinctly one night how a Jap bomber came over—he was at a very high altitude—the searchlights just couldn't find him. However, the 90's fire by Radar, and they got him. We heard him buzzing around up there, and all of a sudden his motor stopped completely. Then it started again, and we could tell that he was trying to gain altitude. He revved the motor several times; finally it died out and down he came with a crash on the coral reefs just out from our area. He burned for a long time thereafter, and the searchlights kept their spots on him.

Summer came and the flowers got underway. A blue water flower on the order of a hyacinth, a red flower with large petals, which I cannot describe, began to bloom. Petunias, morning glories and Easter lilies were bountiful. The breath taking beauty of Gods hand was indescribable in this land that had been so razed by war.

Pine, banana, fig, apple and peach trees grew near places where homes used to be seen. The valleys, rolling hills and ridges that were not torn away, had a deep, shade of green. The rice paddies and gardens, which the people labored so hard in, were as common as our wheat fields at home. Cabbage, carrots and soybeans grew everywhere.

The civilians weren't molested, and the government treated them well. Civilian camps were formed and their men worked for the government. The women went to their gardens daily to pick the food they needed. Okinawans are small and dark skinned from the hot sun. Their women are very ordinary but in among them can be found a pretty girl now and then.

They enjoyed pictures of our girls at home; they liked our candy and cigarettes and laughed at every little thing that seemed to go on. Still others, older no doubt, admired our equipment and gazed about in amazement.

We collected souveigners consisting of helmets, rifles, money, dishware and kimonos, which by the way are very colorful. Trademarks on everything "Japan", of course.

We had gone through one Typhoon several weeks before this, but while we were at Naha Air Field we got hit with another one and it was a doozy. The campaign was over and we had set up a permanent camp, not to far from a huge cave (remember that cave I mentioned?). We had a movie theater and mess hall, all made out of lumber. Rather nice, I might say. In addition we had an area of pyramidal tents on wooden frames that slept four men each . . . All of this was next to the sea wall, which afforded protection from the sea until one day, it took a notion to come ashore.

However, this day and night the sea wall would be no protection at all, because the Typhoon had other ideas of its own. It created such a mess of everything, knocking down the theater, mess hall, and our pyramidal tents with our equipment in them. At the height of the storm we all went into the large cave and stayed for the night, well protected from the storm. What a storm, the Navy lost several ships that capsized and went down. I lost a good friend in one of them. Smaller vessels, Quonset huts that the Army was using and anything else that got in the way were blown all over the island, some of which were placed on shore several hundred feet from where they had been. The 834th wasn't so lucky, the next morning we all came out of the cave and looked at what remained of our equipment . . . all under water. It all had to be renewed and that was my job, being in Battalion Supply. We had to declare the loss of everything else and fill out requisitions for new equipment. Fortunately our motor pool was spared, simply because the trucks, jeeps and half-tracks were just too heavy to be affected by the storm. It was reported that the top winds were hitting 128 miles per hour. I know what that was like because a number of us had to leave the cave and obtain food supplies at the mess hall, which by this time was on the ground. In returning with cartons of supplies, it was almost like crawling, braced against the wind velocity. I got back to the cave ok, but was really soaked and exhausted from the ordeal.

At this time I want to remind you of the cave that I had mentioned earlier that the Japanese had used to hide a large 105 mm howitzer. Well, this was *the*—ave and huge it was. We stayed there for the entire night, not knowing much about what was happening outside.

The next morning as we exited the cave, we were surprised and we knew that we had escaped the fury of the typhoon. Every piece of equipment, tents, mess hall, latrine, you name it, was under water from the night before.

We finally renewed all of our equipment that had been damaged by the typhoon and life took on a different meaning. The Japanese surrendered. We were free to roam about and awaited orders. During the day when we had free time, we would walk out onto the coral and look for seashells. Most of the time we were walking around completely in the nude, enjoying the sunshine, knowing that we were now safe from any destruction.

Korea Bound

It was bad enough, picking up after the typhoon, but that was just a little item in our Army careers. After putting up new tents and making our area presentable again, we thought we were sitting pretty. However, on October 26, 1945, our 'hours of siesta' were broken up when we received our orders to pack up and board ship—we were bound for Korea. T.S., we just missed Japan, the long awaited country of sword swinging nitwits, only to be sent to Korea . . . a land of people, who, we found out later, were very grateful to us for their freedom from the Japanese. This new trip would add a mere thousand miles on our fairly near around the world trip.

What got us was this business of packing. People at home did not enjoy moving, that I could remember; but had they gotten one glimpse of us with all our equipment they would have been amazed. War bond shows were being attended in the states by thousands, who viewed in wonder, the weapons of war and how they reacted to a soldiers touch. Those shows should have given the people in attendance a glimpse of the packing and loading that goes into a troop movement. But, as usual, we complained about anything and everything . . . . no one heard our problems though.

Our convoy of trucks rolled out of our area early in the afternoon, up route 11 to Purple Beach, where we had initially landed. There the Battalion loaded men, vehicles and equipment on several LST's. then came the job of chaining the vehicles to the decks and finding a bunk. That night we had movies on deck and by morning we were steaming for Korea. It was a good feeling to know that these waters were trespassable once again and that the worries of war were over.

We were given lectures on Korea and booklets were passed among us; this being done to familiarize us with what lay ahead and what we should expect. We pictured the people and their habits; laughed at their customs and wondered if we would make friends in time.

There is no need for me to tell about the trip while aboard ship, for anyone who has been at sea, knows that water looks the same, no matter where you see it. However, we did notice the change in climate—the chill air surrounded us, and the sweaters came out. We passed from the China Sea into the Yellow Sea. It was like going over a long dark line stretched out in the water . . . the Yellow Sea holding true to its discription.

From Okinawa we went west toward China. It seemed that the compass never had four points . . . only West, for we followed that reading many a month after leaving Stateside. Several days out saw us heading north. The weather was cold and the sea frowned at us in a gray anger.

A number of days at sea took up our time as we headed for Korea and within an allotted time arrived. It was October 26, 1945. This presented another chance for us, for we were going into another foreign country with occupation on our minds. We set up our camp site, including mess hall, etc. It took a while to unpack and erect our pyramidal tents. Boy, what a difference in the weather . . . . it was going to be cold and we knew it. I stood guard on several occasions and minded the freezing weather very much. When I went off guard duty, I returned to my tent and bunk, piling a single wool blanket, which was G.I. issue, on me plus all my dirty wash which was in a barracks bag, trying to warm up . . . . it was brrrrrrrrr cold. And, that was with all my clothes on. We had a stove inside, but no fuel to burn. Several days later we were supplied with it.

We drove around the area often, to acquire supplies, watching the Korean people as they went about their business each day. They were friendly and on one occasion I and one of my buddies went into Seoul, the capital city. While walking down the street, past a huge wall which surrounded a large oriental looking building; we were greeted by a Korean man and his family. He explained that what we were looking at was a former palace and that he wanted to go inside to view it. However, he could not do so, without a serviceman accompanying him. We volunteered and were indeed glad that we had, for what we viewed was a beautiful oriental pagoda shrine.

The day ended with an invitation to this man's home. His name was Mr. LeeYee Jun. We arrived at his place, promptly removed our boots and were ushered into their living room, while his wife prepared a meal for us. We were seated in another room, on the floor, on pillows. Mr. Lee's wife served us, bringing a small table with 3 place settings on it, filled with rice, a small fish much like anchovies and tea. It was really delightful and to think that we, US soldiers, were being treated like royalty. They were, indeed, thankful for our arriving and chasing out the Japanese, who had been occupying the Korean peninsila for 40 years. Mr. Lee, by the way, was employed by the Chosen National Bank as a teller. We never saw him again after that.

We had several other happenings after that, but our job was to occupy this country until they got back on their feet and I for one was anxious to get discharged and go home. It was an education and a trip paid by Uncle Sam.

About four months later, February 18, 1946, we boarded ship and headed for the Seattle Port of Debarkation, arriving there at 2 PM on March 5, 1946. We stood on the wharf waiting for train transportation while the Red Cross passed out a quart of milk to each man. What a relief to be home on U.S. soil . . . . enough to cry over, I'll say.

THE LAST BIG SWEAT....
AND OUT!

We arrived at Fort Dix Separation Center on the evening of Tuesday, March 12, 1946 at 6:00 PM and as the train pulled to a stop in front of a large wharehouse, the loudspeakers began blaring away. "Do not detrain from train until told to do so". And so we waited. Finally the word came, that we should detrain, and report to room so-and-so. This we did, and upon entering we found it to be a very large room, all set up with desks, microphones and personnel just waiting for us to go through the line, and shove us through to our homes. Although we were tired after the long trip across the country, we were indeed glad to once again get under way and after the night was over we found ourselves much closer to the little white piece of paper which spelled "freedom".

We had to fill out a certain number of forms, and turn in certain pieces of clothing. We ate a light lunch in one of the large mess halls, and were taken to our barracks by bus. There we found no fire, no shower, and no hot water—but there were clean sheets, and new blankets that were to be put on nice mattress' with springs under them. We felt the urge to wash up, and although the water was cold, it was invigorating in itself. Then came sack time. We had dreams that night to be sure.

In order to be discharged, we had to have our names put on a roster; so the next morning we were all out by the bulletin board nosing around the roster that was already put up, looking for our names. Somehow or other we just thought that our names had to be up there on that certain day, but they weren't. We visited the PX, and hung around the barracks trying not to get restless—but to no avail. That night we went up to

The Hands of Time

the Telephone Exchange and made phone calls. I was not able to get in touch with my family for some reason, while others had better luck. They were able to talk with family and tell them that they were home for sure. "I'll be home in a few days"; and many other phrases held deep, found their way from their lips. It was indeed good.

The long white barracks were familiar. A veteran could find his way about a barracks blindfolded. Against the wall before the stairway to the second floor was the drinking fountain, beside it the bulletin board.

Two steps down from the front door was the latrine, with its eight washbowls under the long steel-plated mirror, and six toilets aligned in the corner. On both floors of the barracks were the steel bunks, lined up, with the empty No. 10 cans, used as ashtrays, lined up between them.

The grounds leading up to the barracks were hard-packed now by tens of thousands of men who had marched over them in drill and policed them of cigarette butts at seven o'clock in the morning. On the quadrangle facing the barracks, companies of recruits had formed for a thousand roll calls at reveille, standing at cold attention, and again at retreat, tired from the day's drill, watching the sun set and the first sergeant march stiffly to the head of the company and report, "All present or accounted for," and the flag go down while the band played a loud Star-Spangled Banner.

But now the bands were gone and the sun had set quietly, without official recognition. The lights went on in the barracks and most of us stayed near our bunks, just in case something turned up. We stayed there waiting, not wanting to challenge luck, not wanting to talk about it. We smoked. We got up and walked around. We sat down. We looked at our watches. By eight o'clock the barracks was about as relaxed as a ready room before a mission over Tokyo, or a Higgins boat on its way to Okinawa.

Across the way, a few men were playing poker over a blanket-covered bunk, quietly, as if they were listening for someone to call their names. My buddies—a few—were around me, and we talked over the things that we were going to do first when we entered the door of our homes. We all had the same ideas, but we knew, too, that when the time came to say all that we had planned these many months, our mouths would open, and the words wouldn't come out. Just the same way, did our phone calls, attend themselves.

In the quadrangle at 6:15 each morning, several thousand men were sweating out the breakfast chow line. It was a polite and orderly line—I never saw one like it in this war. Although most of us were still restless and tense, no one bucked for position and no one pulled rank. Beribboned and battlestarred veterans took their places quietly, and even the master sergeants marched along, getting no special privilege.

In the mess hall as in the mess line, the day of the dogface had passed. Those of us who began our Army lives as kitchen police were comforted by the signs on the garbage and refuse cans at the mess hall door. With victory in Europe, black German script had replaced familiar English labels, changing one garbage can from "Nonedible" to "Nicht Essbar," another from "Trap Grease" to "Unnutzliches Fett."

Inside the mess hall, performing the duties of KP, were German prisoners, captured from Tunisia to the Reich. Armed now with ladles and spatulas instead of burp guns and Lugers, the Germans were dishing out breakfast with a flourish.

Back in the barracks we had to listen to a voice that came cackling over the loud speaker system every hour of the day. "Before you get processed, your name's got to be on a roster. If you get processed, you might get out. But if your name's not on a roster, you won't get processed".

One night we returned from chow, and found several hundred men already scanning the rosters for their names. "That's it!" a young corporal shouted, and then stood there admiring his name until he was pushed aside. Others discovered their names, and walked away with broad smiles. We all headed for the telephone exchange once again in order to let our families know when we would be home.

With our names posted, we felt better. The Army now officially recognized we were here and, several of us reasoned, the Army would now be obliged to discharge us.

The voice occasionally raised itself over our barracks-room discussion with orders for other barracks. It faded and squawked, and began in a personal tone. "Will Sergeant Joseph P. Kapatera report to Operations?" "It's good, Kapatera. In to Operations, J. P. Kapatera; you won't be sorry, kid!"

Again the voice spoke, "Let's go, rosters 57 to 68! Out to your posts on the double!"

In the rain-swept quadrangle, our guide, a short, dark haired kid, called off our names and then led us to the post theater for orientation—orientation for civilian life. On the auditorium stage, facing us stood an Army lieutenant. He read from a handful of notes, and explained what was to follow in the next two days.

He reminded us that Army vocabularies were not altogether suited for the family dinner table. "If you want the salt," he said, "Just ask for the salt." It was an old Army joke, but it went over big.

The first requirement of a discharged soldier, said the looey, was to take off his Army clothes and put on civvies; his second, to report to the draft board. "Some of you will want to go out and hit the first bar room you see just to celebrate". "Don't do that." "Go home first." He said, "Until you reach those front porch steps, Uncle Sam has his arm around you; after that he lets go". "So for Gods sake, don't fall down the steps and break your neck." Then the lecture ended, and we walked back to our barracks.

That afternoon we went to see our counselors—enlisted men selected for their experience in personnel problems—were closeted in booths along both walls. They were assigned to advise us on the problems of civilian life, ranging from the conversion of Army life insurance to the payment of taxes, from getting jobs to arranging for Government loans.

That night was spent up at the PX and walking around camp a while.

Next morning our roster was called out to formation, and our guide took us to another barracks where Army doctors were waiting to give us our final physical examination. This was one time that we didn't want to flunk, for if anything was found wrong, we could be held there, until it was made right.

After the physical, we were released for lunch. Our guide informed us that the final formation was scheduled for two-thirty in the afternoon, and that, until then, we could do whatever we liked. Most of us decided, conservatively, to go back to our barracks and sit on our bunks, just in case.

We could hear the voice talking to arrivals over an amplifier in the next barracks. "All men who reported in last night will consult the rosters now posted in the quadrangle," it was saying. "If your names are up, stand by." Already, we were veterans even of the separation center.

Then the voice ordered us to fall in at our posts, take along our baggage and wait for our guide. "This time, men," said the voice, "it's the real thing!"

Our guide set a slow cadence to the supply room, and we crowded up behind him, almost walking on his heels. Facing the supply clerks, we dumped out our last Army possessions. A clerk took my sweater and a pair of khaki trousers.

We were hurried from there into a little building where a dozen Negro girls were sewing patches, stripes and discharge emblems on our uniforms. They handed them back to us, and again we moved on. We signed our discharge papers, scrawling our names for the tension was mounting each minute. We stopped at the door to get our thumbprints stamped on the discharge papers. Our guide led us off to the finance office, where we waited until our names were called. At the cashier's window we received Government checks for our back pay, plus $100 as the first installment of our mustering out pay, plus enough funds to buy railroad tickets home.

Lining up in columns of twos, we marched down the black macadam road to the Fort Dix Chapel, checking our neckties to be sure they were properly tucked in between our second and third shirt buttons. When we reached the chapel door, an organ was playing softly. Quietly we filed into the pews. The chaplain who had spoken to us two days before from the auditorium stage now stood at the altar waiting for us to be seated. The organ stopped and he asked us to rise while he said a prayer. Then he sat down, and next to him an infantry major got up and began speaking. Beside the major, a corporal was waiting with an armful of manila envelopes.

The major spoke and the chapel organ began playing again, cushioning his words. He spoke of past battles and of victory, of the citizen army and how it was formed, of the part the individual had taken, so that the majority might succeed. What he was saying blended with the organ music and the heavy breathing of the men. Men were nervously fingering their brows and chins as the service drew to a close.

The major's words seemed to fade and we began thinking our own valedictories, calling up old names and places. There was that stretch of road from Naha to Shuri where the boys had been convoying with trucks, when a bunch of snipers opened up on them. And the bloody

The Hands of Time

mud of Kakaza Ridge that held to a guys foot when he tried to run and advance. There were many thoughts of those who were not here today.

But we were here, and through the dim lights of the chapel, and soft tones of the organ, came the blast of a horn on a bus, waiting to take us to Philadelphia.

"All of you have one thing in common," the major was saying, putting away his notes. "You served your country in her hour of need. Be as proud of her as she is of you."

The corporal began reading off the names on the Manila envelopes and handing them to the major. We came to attention and saluted for the last time. The major saluted in turn, gave us our envelops, then shook our hands and said, "Good Luck." I figured we'd had it.

I walked out to the bus, thinking about all that had happened in these last 31 months and wondered what I would do with myself now. Family awaited, but I had not talked to them or left them know of my arrival. I had no contact with them at all, simply because I did not know where to call them. My mother had moved to another place and at this hour of the day, my brother and family were not at home. So, I played it by ear. The bus took us to Philadelphia and while there I boarded a train to Phillipsburg, NJ. The train happened to be the milk stop limited and it stopped at every little nook and cranny on the map. It took forever to arrive at my destination.

Finally it happened . . . . P'burg was just ahead. I guess I was a little anxious. I grabbed my duffle bag, walked down the aisle, down the steps, out into the Lehigh Valley and my hometown of Easton across the river. I walked across the bridge and started up Northampton Street. Things were pretty much the same as when I had left, although there were some changes here and there.

As I began to pass the front of Hotel Easton, I had to cross a side street next to it. I was intent on doing something, I don't know what, at the time, when I heard a loud voice yelling "Darrell". I turned and there was my brother Homer who had been working about a block away with the Water Department. He ran like there was no tomorrow, grabbing me and yelling in my ear, saying how glad he was to see me. What a coincidence that those events took place in that order. He didn't have any idea that I was getting discharged or when or where it would happen. I simply had no way of telling my family.

Home At Last

All those days, all those miles, all the waiting was finally over, I was home at last, in Easton, my hometown. My mother was working at Orr's department store at this time and was living on north 12th street in a room. I eventually got to see her and she cried and was so happy that her son had come home from the war . . . . but, she said, "My son is different now, he went away a young youth, now he is a Man". Needless to say, she and I had some really good times together and tried to make up for lost time.

But at this same time, I had another girl in my life that was waiting also. You will just have to imagine how it was when I first saw her. I never saw anyone that looked so pretty. I was waiting in the living room of her parents home and finally she came downstairs (we had a big date planned) . . . . whoopee! I'm telling you that I can still see her and she was the most beautiful thing that I had seen in sometime . . . . I was home and had all kind of ideas . . . good ideas, that is. She was and is the best thing that ever happened to me.

Of course, life went on and I needed to get a job. I went back to Taylor-Wharton where I was working before entering the service. The job that was supposed to be held for me was taken by a gal and I was given a job out in the shop section named Pittsburgh Testing Laboratory. I worked there for several weeks, but was not satisfied and due to that decided to look elsewhere. Many GI's had come home and the country was still cranking out lots of good things in its factories. I was able to get a job under a job training program that the government made available, but I did not last there very long . . . it just wasn't what I was looking for. Eventually I got a job at Mack Printing Company in Easton and I worked there for 40 years before retiring. It was a good place to work and we were able to buy a house because of it.

Our Marriage

The beautiful girl, now a woman, Betty, became my wife on August 30, 1947 and we settled down in an upstairs apartment on Spruce Street. The rent charged was $27.50 per month, which included sharing the bath. I purchased a car which sat out front in all kinds of weather. The street was narrow and it took a bit of maneuvering to park; and when it snowed it was a jig saw puzzle.

So, here we were, in our first apartment, which required a great deal of painting. I accomplished this tremendous amount of work each day during the daylight hours because I was working on the night shift. I thought that I would never get the job finished.

We eventually moved from there, into an apartment at 1153 Lehigh Street. We had made arrangements with a Mrs. Roberts, who owned the property, to move in and fix up. We fixed up for sure. The former tenants had raised chickens in the backyards, repaired cars in the street, raised dogs in the basement, and just made a big nuisance of themselves, as far as the neighbors were concerned. Mrs. Genua, who lived next store, was very happy when we moved in.

We painted and papered the whole apartment. The bathroom had been painted a dark green, including the outside of the tub . . . . we started there. The enclosed back porch had been used to store automobile parts and was rather dirty and full of grease. The basement was filled with scraps of wood and because of that I purchased a circular saw. I was busy cutting lumber for some time. In addition to all of this, I started a fenced in vegetable garden and I must tell you that it was the best garden I ever had . . . . due to plenty of "Hinkel Dreckt".

The Hands of Time

These were very happy years. Betty and I were young and challenged with many projects. The neighbors were very friendly. As tenants, one of our responsibilities were to take care of the fire, which kept the upstairs neighbors warm and satisfied.

During these years, 1951 became a special year for us . . . our son, Kevin, was born on October 11th, of that year and our life took on a different meaning. Each day was spent taking care of him, the newest member of our family. Christmas and other special days were spent in a different way. He was our new addition and we spent a good deal of time enjoying him.

During my youth I took a liking to the piano and as a result, I took piano lessons. This led to a love for music which was built in, I assume. Having this knowledge led me to have a desire to play the organ. Our church had an old Estey Organ which had seen its day somewhat. Eventually the organist retired and left an opening for me, which I promptly attempted to fill. After obtaining a teacher and taking lessons, I became the official organist of 1st Church on 10th Street in Easton. This required playing for two services each Sunday as well as directing the choir.

Over time the Estey Organ became so ancient that it had all kinds of problems. The church officials decided to have it renovated and in doing so they found that it had acquired a collection of "coal dust" at the bottom of its pipes. The church had a coal hopper that used "pea coal", with a blower that fired up the furnace. In disassembling the organ the workers found excessive amounts of coal dust. It was cleaned and renovated till it was back in shape again.

It came time for the first use and as I played it, it sounded like it was on its last legs, squealing and working terribly hard. I was convinced that it would never be the same again. Time didn't help at all. It just continued to sound like it had given up entirely.

I talked to the Church Board and after much deliberation at the board meetings, they decided to purchase a new organ. After much discussion and consideration about monies needed, the board decided to go ahead with the decision.

The Board and I went to the Allen Organ Co. and tried out various instruments, finally deciding on a 3-Manual Allen Organ, which pleased me to the utmost. As a result of this final decision, I remained

Organist-Choir Director of the First Evangelical Church for the next 35 years.

During this time period, 1955, our second child was born. A beautiful daughter who we named Vickie Joy, was born to us. What a joy, so her name, arrived at our home. She caused us additional happiness.

My life, at this point, was dedicated to the use of my hands. As I worked at the Mack Printing Co., I became a very proficient Monotype Keyboard Operator. My hands again were in use a great deal of the time. The Keyboard consisted of 279 keys, much like a huge typewriter. We worked under a Bonus System and were paid extra wages for great production. I type 120 words per minute and was a very accurate keyboarder. The proofreaders always would seek my work and people marveled at my ability. My immediate boss did mention one time that he felt that my ability at the piano and organ afforded me much of my technique on the Monotype Keyboard. In fact, one of the employees, who worked in the Composing Room had suggested, several times, that he felt I should have my hands insured. I, however, never did it.

Eventually, our department of hot type, became a thing of the past, as "cold type"—compterization came into the printing world and what a change it was.

I was given the chance one day to make a drastic change. Other employees that had more seniority than I were given the chance to go into the new faze—computerization—and they turned it down. I was called into the front office and given the same opportunity. Without thinking about it twice, I took the chance, because I felt that was the way to go. I was never sorry about my decision. After much learning through mistakes, etc., I ended up training all the keyboarders from our former department . . . it took three years to do so.

During the year of 1960 our third child, a daughter, named Sandra was born and she, being very special, became another beautiful asset to our family. She set the joy bells ringing in our hearts and proved to be a class act with her many different talents.

The company continued to function vey well, with much "overtime" involved in our schedule . . . through the week, and Saturdays and Sundays were very common in our schedule. I worked for them for forty years before retirement and wish that I could do it again.

Back in the early years of our marriage, I read an advertisement in a magazine pertaining to a grandfather clock kit to build. It was a new challenge and I just couldn't turn away from it. I chose a kit of walnut and sent for it. After some time, I received the kit and found it to be very complicated. I had misgivings. Did I do the correct thing? I immediately placed the entire kit under the bed and there it stayed for a long time. One day, after much prodding by my wife, I took it out of its hiding place and proceeded to take it to my workshop. It was indeed a great challenge, however I found that I enjoyed every hour that I spent with it. In doing so, I had also read about the procedure involving "hand rubbing", which I took on myself to do. I actually applied the finish by hand and it turned out "beautiful". It turned out so well that I decided to build another. It was mahogany and it to was beautiful. This clock was given to our oldest daughter. I was so satisfied that I obtained another clock, finished it, hand rubbed it in oak and gave this clock to our youngest daughter. It turned out to be the most beautiful of all three. I must add that these "kits", as they are called, are not all that easy and require a great deal of patience and time. Here was evidence of my "handiness" coming to the surface once again.

These previous years were just the beginning of 63 many wonderful fulfilling ones that challenged our love for each other. Our family grew, with these three beautiful children, a home of our own and a career as Church Organist and Choir Director for a period of 35 years. I wouldn't trade any of it for all the money in the world. I had talent that was discovered in my later life and I was able to put it to good use. God had Blessed with His abundance.

I must add to this challenging personal history; that I don't believe to this day that I would have been able to go through all of this without the help and constant care from my Lord and Savior Jesus Christ in my life. HE, above all else, made things possible for me to stand up to the many temptations placed before me and HE protected me at all times.

Epilogue

The reader must consider the time and place that this writing encompasses, for during World War II the enemy was considered a very worthy opponent who was engaged to win. Thus he was reckless and cruel and could do nothing less than be a worthy opponent. As a result you will read names applied to men who were out to succeed and so the author uses terms that may appear cruel to whomever the reader may be. This nation sought to succeed at all costs and thus it was practiced. Keep these things in mind and remember that all is not contained herein. For the sake of the reader, the author went easy on these matters so as to let them escape the many cruel happenings. History has taken care of this. We know today that this same former enemy, although defeated, is still very much able to practice his many capabilities.